DATE DUE

ILL: 86876446 MAY 15 2018			

HAROLD KLEMP

The CALL *of* SOUL

HAROLD KLEMP

ECKANKAR
Minneapolis
www.Eckankar.org

ABOUT THIS BOOK: *The Call of Soul* is compiled from Harold Klemp's writings and talks. Some of these selections originally appeared in his books published by Eckankar. Others have never appeared in print before. The accompanying CD contains excerpts from his talks, including dream and Soul Travel techniques.

The Call of Soul

Copyright © 2009 ECKANKAR

Printed in USA
Compiled by John Kulick and Doug Munson
Edited by Patrick Carroll, Joan Klemp, and Anthony Moore
Cover photo by Yva Momatiuk and John Eastcott/Minden Pictures
Text photo by Robert Huntley
Cover design by Doug Munson

Library of Congress Cataloging-in-Publication Data
Klemp, Harold.
    The call of soul / Harold Klemp.
      p. cm.
    ISBN 978-1-57043-309-2 (pbk : alk. paper) 1. Eckankar (Organization) 2. Spiritual life—Eckankar (Organization) I. Title.
    BP605.E3K5525 2007
    299'.93—dc22
                                2009033147

∞ This paper meets the requirements of ANSI/NISO Z39.48-1992 (Permanence of Paper).

Contents

INTRODUCTION

*I*f you are a sincere seeker of truth, you realize that something within you is constantly pushing you from the nest. You know the answers you seek do exist somewhere in the world. This inner force that pushes you to find the answers is an urge you have no control over.

It is the call of Soul.

Prayer. Meditation. Contemplation. What's at the heart of these spiritual practices? Each is a response to the call of Soul. Each represents an individual's desire to contact the source of all truth. Different paths to reach the same goal.

You are Soul, a divine spark of God on a journey homeward. Soul wants to experience more of the Voice of God, which can be heard as Sound or seen as Light. This Voice often remains an unconscious inner experience of which the outer, or human, side of the individual is not aware.

You are Soul, a divine spark of God on a journey homeward.

Outwardly, all you know is this gnawing feeling that there is more to life than you have yet discovered. So you begin your search through different philosophies, looking for the missing link.

You have heard the call of Soul and set off in pursuit of God.

1

1

IN PURSUIT OF GOD

A search for happiness is the pursuit of God. Yet the reason so many people fail to find happiness is because they look for it in the wrong place— at the market instead of in their hearts.

It takes discipline to pursue God.

There is no mystery to finding God: just follow the Sound of the divine Voice back home. Could anything be easier? Not so for most people, for whom the pursuit of God is as unlikely as the phenomenon of a flying rabbit. And why? It's simply not in their consciousness yet to know that the destiny of each Soul is to become a Co-worker with God, who expects more of us than an eternity of eating and play.

For many, life is much like a trip to a casino. They place all their talents and dreams on the gaming table then bet the outcome of this life upon a turn of the wheel of fortune. That is the sum of their spiritual life in pursuit of God.

Happiness, to them, is blind luck.

People want happiness, but they go about it backward. They keep looking for happiness. And then they spend their money on things: new computer toys, new cars, new clothes, and the like. Trying to find happiness. If they'd only look for freedom

The destiny of each Soul is to become a Co-worker with God.

first—maybe meditate like the Buddhists or contemplate as we do in Eckankar, which is a lighter form of meditation.

Yet some individuals do have a true desire for God and use some form of prayer or worship to better understand the Creator. Mostly, however, their prayer is like traffic on a one-way street: They do all the talking. It never occurs to them to stop for a moment and listen. God may want to speak.

Often, God doesn't get a word in at all.

How, then, does God communicate with us?

How, then, does God communicate with us? God speaks to all life with the voice of divine Light and Sound. The Christian name for these dual aspects of God is the Holy Spirit, or the Holy Ghost, which in Eckankar we refer to by the age-old name ECK.

The range of vibration in the universe spans from infinity to infinity. And while the primal cause of vibration is the Light and Sound of God, the human voice is a mere speck on the full scale of vibration. Why would God only speak in a whisper? Yet people who believe that God speaks chiefly in the frequency range of the human voice forget that the human voice, in comparison to the universe of sound, is but a tiny whisper.

So the idea that God only speaks to life within the narrow field of human sound is an attempt to reduce the might of God.

The Light and Sound of God are the food and drink of saints. Saul of Tarsus on the road to Damascus was struck to the earth by the Light of

God. Martin Luther, the great reformer, was also for-tunate to see It. Then there was Genghis Khan, the Mongol conqueror of the thirteenth century, who every so often would fall into a swoon for days, able only to chant HU, an ancient name for God. In those trance states, he saw and heard the majestic Light and Sound of God. The Divine One spoke through the Holy Spirit.

So the highest form of speech from God to the more spiritually advanced of the human race is the Light and Sound.

Who, then, does God talk to?

In fact, everyone who has made a contribution to the human race has heard or seen the True Voice. The ways of God are many. God often speaks in a less direct manner to dreamers, poets, visionaries, and prophets—in part, through visions or dreams, daydreams, prayer (the listening kind), or intuition.

Who does God talk to?

History tells of many such people.

Brother Lawrence was a Carmelite monk in Paris around 1666. He was the monk whose duty it was to wash the pots and pans. Brother Lawrence found a way to practice the presence of God while washing the pots and pans, doing even the very lowly jobs. The people around him couldn't really understand how he could be so happy while doing the dirty work. It was because he saw God in every-thing he did.

A list of other famous people who have been a mouthpiece for the Voice of God includes the likes of Socrates, Plato, Elijah, King David, Mozart, Beethoven, Jung, Einstein, Shelley, Edison, Michelangelo, and thousands more. Each does his best to render the divine will into human terms, using a natural genius as the tool of communication.

Each does his best to render the divine will into human terms.

The Sound and Light carry out God's scheme of creation. So the highest anyone can aspire to is a life of high creativity, but always guided by the force of divine love.

That is how to be most like God.

2

YOUR STATE OF
CONSCIOUSNESS
IS YOUR
STATE OF ACCEPTANCE

*A*n individual's state of consciousness simply means his ability to accept change in his life.

It includes new thoughts and new feelings, and the new behavior and actions that will naturally come as a result.

A state of consciousness is also flexible in that it swells (expands) and shrinks (contracts). Some events in our lives make us full of joy and goodwill, another way of saying an expansion of consciousness. Other events leave us suspicious or hostile or gloomy—a contraction. There are temporary changes in one's state of consciousness as well as more long-lasting ones, the sum of all the lesser changes.

So your state of consciousness is a living thing. After all, it is a reflection of you—Soul—and is a product of each and every experience you've ever had. Ever.

Your state of consciousness is a reflection of you—Soul.

Different experiences make for the difference in people.

The human race as a whole also has a state of consciousness, or level of acceptance. This ability does shift with the passage of time. Sometimes it moves ahead spiritually. At other times, there is a shift to a lower state.

ADVANCES IN CONSCIOUSNESS

For example, mankind had made some nice gains in the expansion of its world by the first millennium AD. Let's overlook its never-ending lust for war and conquest, which will endure as long as human passions go unchecked. People had learned to make a record in writing of their exploits so future generations might profit by it if they so chose. A written language made it possible to review past mistakes and go on from there. A few, advanced in consciousness, had set down codes of conduct for society: like the sayings of Confucius, the ten commandments of Moses, the thoughts of Socrates and Plato, to name a few.

Those were signs of mankind's progress in its state of consciousness.

Those were signs of mankind's progress in its state of consciousness.

Yet there were the dark times too. The most glaring example is perhaps the Dark Ages in Europe, usually fixed from the fifth through the tenth century. Some historians claim the only reason to call it a "dark" period is because so little written history survives from then. That is exactly the point. Why is there so little in writing? There was a falling back in consciousness.

But even as late as the seventeenth century, Galileo still felt the sting of the Inquisition, which censored his observation—made with the new invention, the telescope—that not all heavenly bodies revolved around the earth. His support of the Copernican heliocentric system shook the foundations of the Christian Church. It called the theory a heresy.

The Dark Ages reflect a retreat in the state of consciousness.

Every person has a unique state of consciousness, even as does every community, town, city, state, region, country, or continent. The same holds for races, religions, political groups, and every other association that comes to mind. For example, who would say there's no difference in the teachings of Islam and Buddhism? The unique doctrines of each are merely an expression of two different states of consciousness, or the acceptance of certain universal ideas that appeal more to one group than the other.

Every person has a unique state of consciousness, even as does every community, town, city, state, region, country, or continent.

So a state of consciousness is the level of acceptance that one has to changes in conditions.

For some of a certain temperament, blind faith in salvation is a comfort. It gives them courage. They are relieved by the idea that a more advanced spiritual person will take care of all the details when this life comes to an end and will assure them a happy, joyful existence in the hereafter. And that's OK.

People of another state of consciousness may have a more hands-on approach to the issue of death, which punctuates human life for many with a question mark. Their state of consciousness says, "It's up to each of us to find our own salvation."

Is it any wonder that so much of our history is penned in blood? No human state of consciousness is of a shining purity. Each has its stains. These stains are from the five passions of lust, greed, anger, vanity, and an undue attachment to material things. But their state of consciousness does determine how darkly these stains color the behavior of people toward each other.

TRUTH IS EVER NEW

"Seth" was on a flight to Perth, Australia. Beside him was "Edna," returning home to Perth after a visit with relatives in Canada. "This was my last trip to Canada," she told him. "I'm in my seventies now."

When Edna found out Seth had never been to Perth, she was delighted to answer his questions about the climate, culture, and things to do.

"What are you reading?" she inquired, glancing at the book in his hand.

Seth said, *"Soul Travelers of the Far Country.* It's written by the spiritual leader of Eckankar. It's about Soul's journey through this world."

Edna mentioned a number of spiritual paths she had joined at one time or another. "I was always looking for a certain element of truth, but I never found it," she said sadly. "Finally, I just gave up and quit all religions. I came to the conclusion that this day-to-day existence is all I can expect from life. Now I'm just putting in my time until it's over."

Yet she was curious about his spiritual path and started asking some questions. Seth explained that the teachings of Eckankar are based on the Light

"What are you reading?" she inquired. Seth said, "It's about Soul's journey through this world."

and Sound. He also told her about HU, the sacred name for God, which we often sing during our spiritual exercises. "The reason I'm going to Perth is to attend an Eckankar seminar," he said.

Edna was interested, but at this point in her life she felt she was too old to renew her search.

"Soul has no age," said Seth. "It doesn't matter when you begin to look for truth. It's beyond age and time. It makes no difference whether you would have found it in your teens, or whether you find it now in your seventies. Truth is ever new. When you are ready, it will find you."

His words made sense to her. All of a sudden she was struck by the timing of the situation. On a flight back from what was to be her last trip to Canada, she had found herself seated next to Seth. He was going to an Eckankar seminar in her hometown of Perth, of all places. It occurred to her how fully and completely this ECK works. She was grateful to finally have heard about It.

"Soul has no age," said Seth. "It doesn't matter when you begin to look for truth. When you are ready, it will find you."

A Capacity to Accept Change

People relate to a given set of conditions in keeping with their capacity to accept change, as said earlier. But how does this ability come about?

Human joy and suffering in everyday life are always on hand, to build and shape our outlook on the events that face us without end. Experience leads us to love and compassion. A child may carry into adulthood the memory of a grandmother, on one side of the family, who was gentle, good, and kind. Yet its memory of the other grandmother may be quite the opposite. The second grandmother, about the same age as the first, leaves behind a memory of telling bawdy jokes, embarrassing the clergyman, and taking life with a wink.

It's all about two states of consciousness.

How open, loving, and forgiving are we? ECK Master Rebazar Tarzs* says, "Purity calls for the highest within man. You cannot slander nor can you see the evil in others" (*Stranger by the River,* "Purity").

Ah, but we should also note what he adds: "Dwell upon the good within thy neighbor and thus you will exalt the good in him, and bring out the good in thyself." That is also a form of spiritual exercise.

Now you should have a better idea about your own state of consciousness, for it is nothing more than the amount of love you can accept from God.

And give love as it has been given to you.

Your own state of consciousness is nothing more than the amount of love you can accept from God.

---

*The ECK Masters are spiritual guides people have looked to since the beginning of time for guidance, protection, and divine love.

3

Discover
the Source
of All Truth

*L*earn to go inside yourself, because this is the source of all truth. There are a lot of holy temples out here, but the most sacred of all is the temple inside you, because this is where you meet with the Holy Spirit.

How do you meet with the Holy Spirit?

If you're in Christianity, you pray. You come to the holy temple, to the holy of holies, through prayer. You meet on holy ground with your God. If you're a member of any other religion, you have a means of going to that holy of holies, whether it's meditation or contemplation or prayer.

Go to the holy of holies. It's the temple inside you. This is the place where all truth comes from. Before there were words, before there was a written Bible or a printed Gutenberg Bible, before there was Luther's translation, there was the Word in the heart of mankind.

This is the temple. Go there.

Learn to go
inside yourself,
because this is
the source of
all truth.

THY WILL BE DONE

There is a true way to pray, and that way is simply to say, "Thy will be done." Because it will be done anyway. Even better, perhaps, be silent and let God speak to you.

The Spindrift Organization has done a lot of experiments in the lab trying to prove that prayer works. They set up experiments with plants, and they tried directed prayer. They'd always have a control group. Then they would see if there were any differences in plant growth. And there were.

They did these experiments for a while, and then somebody had an idea. They said, "We've proved now that prayer changes things." In other words, saying to the little plant, "Grow!" "But now let's see if there's a difference between directed prayer and other types." They wanted to look at another kind of prayer, which is *nondirected* prayer.

Nondirected prayer is more along the lines of "Thy will be done."

So they took a plate with mold on it. And they put it through a quick rinse of alcohol to give the mold a shock, to almost kill it. And then they drew a line right down the center.

They did other experiments and got the same results: the nondirected prayer was better than telling God what to do.

Side A was the control side. They wouldn't pray for that side. They asked people to pray for the mold on side B, but not on the order of, "Grow, you little green molds, grow!" They didn't do it like that. They just said, "Thy will be done," regarding the B side.

By doing this truly, people are giving goodwill to life. They're passing along the love of God to other people and things.

They found that nondirected prayer worked even better than directed prayer. Then they did other experiments and got the same results: the nondirected prayer was better than telling God what to do. They also found that some kind of attention was better than nothing at all.

It gets very difficult when you try to direct things. For example, if you have an illness and say, "God, I need more red blood cells. Produce more red blood cells." That may be exactly the wrong thing. You might need more white blood cells.

Directed prayer doesn't work as well because it depends upon the human consciousness and all its ignorance. But nondirected prayer depends upon the divine power, the higher power. It depends upon the power of God. So whether you say, "Thy will, not mine be done," or "May the blessings be," this is the proper spiritual way to direct your own life.

So whether you say, "Thy will, not mine be done," or "May the blessings be," this is the proper spiritual way to direct your own life.

You can use it in your own spiritual exercises with a word that you sing to yourself during contemplation (HU is a good one—see page 36). You can sing the word, but before you start, you can say, "May the blessings be" or "Thy will be done."

If you have a health problem, or if you're having a problem finding work or keeping the job you have, or if you're having a problem with your loved one or someone not so loved—instead of saying, "God, help me be stronger," maybe just try "Thy will be done."

It's unconditional love that makes such a prayer. And this is important.

What many people don't realize is that God's love, too, is unconditional love. Soul exists because

God loves It. That means you exist because God loves you.

4

LEARN TO LISTEN

Correct prayer is listening to God. If a person is going to err in prayer, it's through too much telling or talking to God. There's nothing wrong with talking to God. But after you've asked your question, listen. Be quiet and listen.

Most people are used to prayers that ask something of God. They are used to telling God, "Do this for me. I want health. My finances aren't going very well; I need wealth."

Everybody's always telling God what to do. Then they wonder, *Does God get sick of listening? Why doesn't God ever do anything?*

If we shut our eyes in contemplation, listen, and wait for God to speak to us, we begin to see how listening is true prayer, prayer of the highest sort. Mostly, true prayer is listening to God.

True prayer is listening to God.

It is a whole different approach. Through spiritual exercises and this contemplative effort, we learn to listen to the Voice of God. The Voice of God is the Holy Spirit, which we call the ECK.

LISTENING TO GOD'S GUIDANCE SAVES LIVES

Deboee was a pilot on a DC-9 passenger plane. One day the plane was flying out of Abidjan, Ivory

Coast, with a full load of passengers, and they had an emergency during takeoff. They were headed for Monrovia, Liberia, which was to the west.

Suddenly there was a violent vibration. The co-pilot was flying, and Deboee said, "Go with the take-off." The other choice would have been to abort. This was how the pilots' guidelines read. With the copilot flying, Deboee was very receptive to the Mahanta, to the Inner Master*, and he listened for any guidance that might come.

Deboee kept listening, and in some cases he did the wrong thing by the book. But it saved everybody's life.

Now followed a series of life-or-death decisions. Deboee kept listening, and in some cases he did absolutely the wrong thing by the book. But it saved everybody's life.

First was the decision to continue with the take-off or not, and aborting meant they would have ended up in the sea. And he said, "Lives were saved right there."

Deboee knew there was a tire problem, so he didn't retract the undercarriage because that would have damaged the hydraulic system. Later, the Abidjan air traffic control center confirmed that they had left part of a tire on the runway.

Now came the decision to divert to Accra, in Ghana. This was well to the east. With the under-carriage down, the extra drag meant there would be too little fuel to reach the original destination of Monrovia. Fuel consumption would have been twice

---

*An expression of the ECK, or Holy Spirit

as much, and they would never have made it.

Then on the way to Accra, the engine on the same side as the burst tire developed an oil leak. The procedure said to shut down the engine. But the plane was overloaded. And with the undercarriage down, there was all this drag.

A DC-9 has two engines. And if he had shut the engine down, one engine alone couldn't keep the plane airborne. That would have been it. All lives lost.

Deboee brought the throttle back to idle just to see what would happen, and the plane lost altitude. So he had to choose here. He brought the throttle back up, pushed it forward, and they regained altitude. They kept flying in spite of the oil leak. And how did Deboee make these decisions? Well, the Mahanta had given him a nudge—had said to do exactly what he'd done.

How did Deboee make these decisions?

So now came the question: should he announce to the passengers what kind of a stew they're in? And he realized, no, they'd panic, and they already have enough problems.

He just said, "We've got a tire problem, and we'll be landing at Accra." And the people were very calm. Once the DC-9 was over Accra, it had used up enough fuel to be well within a safe landing weight. They shut down the engine with the oil leak, and they made a perfect landing. Everyone was safe. Deboee credited this guidance 100 percent to the Mahanta. Deboee said that just a single wrong decision would have spelled disaster.

Deboee drew a parallel to other people who listened to the inner voice.

Then he added something very interesting. Deboee drew a parallel to other people who listened to the inner voice. He said Bach, Beethoven, Mozart, Handel, and Tchaikovsky, to name a few, were all vehicles who listened to this inner guidance and acted. And we are all witness to the result of their listening. We can all hear the results through the music they wrote. Just a beautiful connection.

5

THE POWER OF CHANTING

$\mathcal{S}$ome time ago there was a Benedictine monastery in France. The Benedictines are known for their very rigorous schedule of prayer, work, and chanting. They chant from six to eight hours a day, work very hard, and only sleep a little.

This particular monastery got a new abbot. While trying to bring in the reforms of the Second Vatican Council, he made a study of the chanting the monks did.

While trying to bring in reforms, a new abbot made a study of the chanting the monks did.

Eventually the abbot told the monks, "We're chanting from six to eight hours a day. This time could be better spent for something else." And he asked them to stop chanting.

In just a few weeks, the abbot noticed that the monks looked very fatigued. Everyone was so tired that they could barely continue with their daily schedule. Some thought maybe the fatigue was from working such long hours and getting so little sleep. So the abbot gave them eight instead of four hours of sleep and reduced their workload.

When the fatigue persisted, a medical specialist and a dietitian were called in. They prescribed more meat and potatoes instead of the monks' centuries-old diet of fish and vegetables. Now they not only felt more fatigue, but many of the monks became ill.

Seeing that none of this was working, the abbot

finally called in a man who studied sound.

Since this man knew that certain sounds were very beneficial, he told the monks, "Go back to chanting six to eight hours a day. Chanting is what heals you and gives you the strength to keep up your schedule."

The monks began chanting again. They resumed their simple diet and only got four hours of sleep. Within six months, most of them were back on their rigorous schedule, fit as ever.

The chant of HU gets the same job done in just twenty minutes.

Most of us don't have the time or inclination to live in a monastery and chant six to eight hours a day. The chant of HU is a higher chant, and it gets the same job done in just twenty minutes.

Chanting HU is what gives Soul vitality and strength.

A CALL FOR HELP

A seeker I'll call Peter attended an Eckankar workshop in Switzerland. He told the story of how, within a year, his wife left him and his son committed suicide. He had totally given up, and he went into the woods to do the same thing as his son. He said, "What have I got to live for? My wife's gone, my son is gone. Everything I loved, all gone."

Then he thought, *Well, God, I'll give you one more chance*. He said, "God, if you exist, I need a sign right now." Then he made some kind of a deal with God that he didn't talk about.

Well, the veil opened up between the world of the living and the world of those living beyond this world. You notice I didn't say the dead, but those living beyond. Because everything is life. This world is separated from the others by a veil, and Peter was able to see through it. Mercifully, he was able to see what would be his lot as a suicide. It wasn't a happy one.

Ten minutes later a voice spoke to him, "Are you making your decision in favor of God, or against yourself?" That took him quite by surprise.

Peter had studied all different kinds of religions. He'd done chants of all sorts. He'd chanted om and gotten no help. One day he was passing by a little church, and a voice said to him, "Stay a little." So he went inside. When service was done, he went outside and sat on the grass. And Jesus appeared to him.

As Peter told all this to the people at the Eckankar workshop, he asked, "Why Jesus? He wasn't exactly my favorite master." But it was Jesus. Jesus took him by the hand, and this great love passed between them.

THE POWER OF HU, A LOVE SONG TO GOD

When he finished his story, Peter just sat there, and the room was quiet. Finally someone said, "We can't help you with a solution to your problem. But we can tell you about the HU song, the love song to God. It's a mantra above all others."

So Peter learned about the HU song. The HU song, this beautiful HU song, you can sing individually or in a group. When you do, you're lifting yourself spiritually. It's not to change another's state of

You can sing the HU song individually or in a group. When you do, you're lifting yourself spiritually.

consciousness, because that's black magic.

I know that's cutting the definition of black magic very fine, but whenever you try to change another to your way of thinking, or your state of consciousness, through prayer or in some other way, that's black magic. And in this respect, black magic and white magic are the same. Some people try to separate the two, but it comes down to changing somebody else's life without his permission. That is black magic, and it is a violation of spiritual law for which the violator must someday pay.

Changing somebody else's life without his permission is a violation of spiritual law.

LET IT BE

So "Ann," one of the ECK facilitators, had this very strong urge to help Peter, but the Inner Master's voice came to her and said, "Let it be."

Ann was driving home after that session, when the Beatles song "Let It Be" came on the car radio. The first words go like this:

> When I find myself in times of trouble
> Mother Mary comes to me
> Speaking words of wisdom, let it be.
> And in my hour of darkness
> She is standing right in front of me
> Speaking words of wisdom, let it be.
> Let it be, let it be.
> Whisper words of wisdom, let it be.

Then Ann understood. Peter was a sheep from another fold. He belonged with Jesus because that was his state of consciousness. He had to complete a few more courses before he'd be ready for the college of ECK. And now she understood.

That night, Ann's heart was filled with gladness. Her job had simply been to set up the workshop, to give the presentation so this man could make contact with the ECK teachings. Someday when Peter is ready to take another spiritual step, he would know about ECK. Meanwhile, he has received the gift of the HU song, which brings spiritual upliftment.

It's a Miracle!

Katie is an acupuncturist. Patients who feel their condition isn't improving will sometimes ask her, "Isn't there something else, something more that I can do?" So Katie will check with the Mahanta, her inner guide, to find out if she should speak about the HU song.

So Katie will check with the Mahanta, her inner guide, to find out if she should speak about the HU song.

One of her patients was Jessica. And Katie had the nudge to share the HU song with her. Now Jessica is in her sixties. She had polio as a child, and most of her life she was under heavy medication. She'd often sleep twenty hours a day.

Jessica's doctor and Katie were both trying to get Jessica free from her medication. And when Jessica began to sing HU along with the treatments she was getting, suddenly her condition improved vastly.

Jessica said, "It's like a miracle." And Katie observed, "That's how Divine Spirit changes lives."

Jessica has a housemate by the name of Linda. "She's always going a mile a minute," Jessica said about Linda. Katie, just wondering, said, "Do you suppose Linda might be helped with meditation?"

Jessica said, "Oh, we sing HU together. In fact, Linda likes it so much she's inviting friends over so they can all sing HU together on Sunday."

HU opens the heart to healing and draws one closer to God. It's easy to do this simple spiritual exercise.

What's interesting is that Katie has seen such a correlation between the openness of Soul—especially one who embraces and uses the HU—and the patient's correspondent healing and upliftment in consciousness.

And it is so, because HU opens the heart to healing.

SING HU TO OPEN YOUR HEART

Singing HU draws one closer to God. It's easy to do this simple spiritual exercise.

With eyes open or closed, take a few deep breaths to relax. Then begin to sing HU (*pronounced hue*) in a long, drawn out sound, HU-U-U-U. Take another breath, and sing HU again. You can continue for up to twenty minutes.

If you sing HU with a feeling of love, it will gradually open your heart to God.

To learn more about HU, and to hear the heart-opening sound of thousands of Souls singing this beautiful, powerful love song to God, listen to the CD included at the back of this book.

6

THE TRANSFORMING POWER OF THE SPIRITUAL EXERCISES OF ECK

*B*eyond prayer is contemplation.

Contemplation is a method that enables you to begin to go out and actively explore the inner worlds of your own being. It is different than meditation, a passive state in which the practitioner goes within and quietly waits for the light.

Explore the inner worlds of your own being.

If you have never used contemplation or a spiritual exercise before, and you would like to compare it to prayer, then pray in the evening before you go to bed, and try a spiritual exercise later. You can look to Jesus or anyone else while following the instructions given for "A Simple Spiritual Exercise to Try" on page 44 or any of the other spiritual exercises included in this book. Try it for yourself and see if there is a difference between how prayer works for you and how a spiritual exercise works for you.

GAINING SPIRITUAL STRENGTH

Many years ago I read the story of Milo of Croton, who became known as the strongest man in his country. He began to build his strength by walking the streets of ancient Greece with a baby calf perched on his back. With each passing day the animal grew a little bit bigger, a little bit heavier.

But because Milo kept up the practice every day, he barely noticed it. His strength increased proportionately, so that at no point was the weight too much for him to carry. By the time the calf grew into a full-size bull, Milo was acknowledged as the strongest man in Croton.

This, in effect, is how the Mahanta helps the student of ECK to build strength. It starts with a little bit of truth given each day, like carrying a baby calf. Then you get a little bit more and a little bit more. As you move on in the initiations of Eckankar (sacraments that mark spiritual awakenings), you grow increasingly stronger, until finally your spiritual strength becomes more than anyone could imagine.

Milo liked to challenge the other men by closing his hand around a pomegranate and daring anyone to take it from him. The others would try to pry his hand open, squeezing and pulling on his fingers with all their might. Only when they finally gave up would he release his grip. He'd hold out his hand to display an unbruised pomegranate. This feat not only proved his great strength, but also his ability to control it.

The Spiritual Exercises of ECK give you confidence in yourself. You learn that you are Soul, you are eternal.

Spiritual strength is not the kind that needs to be shown off; one can be gentle or weak in the body yet strong in Spirit.

The Spiritual Exercises of ECK give you confidence in yourself. You learn that you are Soul, you are eternal. Then you know with certainty that you live forever, that death cannot destroy you.

The spiritual exercises work similarly to physical exercises. If you want your body to be strong and healthy, you've got to swim or run or do something to keep fit. For the Soul body, you do the Spiritual Exercises of ECK, a form of inner communication also called contemplation.

These spiritual exercises link you with the guidance of the Holy Spirit, which is seen as Light and heard as Sound. The inner Sound is the Voice of God calling us home. The inner Light is a beacon to light our way. All the Spiritual Exercises of ECK are built on these two divine aspects of the Holy Spirit.

These spiritual exercises link you with the guidance of the Holy Spirit, which is seen as Light and heard as Sound.

A CHANGE IN CONSCIOUSNESS

Myra has two grandsons. One Saturday morning, they came over to visit. "Mark" is the older; he is thirteen. "Jimmy" is eleven.

Myra loves them dearly, so she joyfully greeted them. Then she said, "But it's just about time for my spiritual exercises. You're free to stay out here or go to the den and watch cartoons on TV." They said, "No. No. We want to do a spiritual exercise with you." So Myra said, "OK."

They all went into her bedroom and sat on her bed. "All right," she said. "Look for the Light, and listen for the Sound. Look into your Spiritual Eye."

It wasn't five minutes before she heard snickering. Myra opened one eye. She's been around. She peeked. She saw the younger grandson, Jimmy, sitting with his hand covering his mouth, laughing.

At the same time, Mark, the older boy, was whispering in one of those stage whispers intended for Grandma's ears, no doubt. "She's making it up," he said. "She's making it up."

This aggravated Grandma. She said, "You all get out of here and let me do my spiritual exercise." She's from the South, and she doesn't mess around.

Laughing and snickering, the boys left the room, and Myra sat there by herself. She likes her special HU session because of the love that comes through from the Mahanta. She feels all this love. So she settled in and began the spiritual exercise.

She was just getting into it, when she heard a very gentle knocking on the door. She opened her eyes, rolling them to the ceiling, and said, "What is it?"

Mark said, "Can I sing the HU with you? It calms me down and makes me feel better."

Mark, the older of the two, crept in, knowing he shouldn't be doing this. He said, "Can I do your spiritual exercise with you? Can I sing the HU with you? It calms me down and makes me feel better."

"OK," said Myra. "But this time I'll walk you through it with an imaginative technique. And you can take it from there."

So Mark sat down. And, as Myra tells it, "Like an old hen with one chick, I put my wing around his shoulders, and we started to sing HU."

After awhile, Myra became quiet. Then she described aloud the scene they were to visualize. She said, "We're walking on a beach. Feel the sun's warmth on your body." She took him through this spiritual exercise very nicely, step-by-step.

"Notice the wind blowing a breeze that plays with our hair. The silky sand is squishing between our toes. Notice the smell and sound of ocean waves rolling in to shore to kiss the sand at our feet." Very much the poet.

"And look," she said. "There's a sailboat appearing on the horizon. Look, it's coming to shore, and there's the Mahanta at the tiller."

She described climbing into the boat, and the Mahanta sailing the boat to an island with a beautiful crystal castle on it. Then Myra stopped talking and they sat quietly. They were listening, listening, still on the edge of the bed.

Then Mark said, "Uh, Grandma, what color is that light?"

Then Mark said to her in a soft voice, "Uh, Grandma, what color is that light?"

Myra's very down-to-earth. "What color do you see?"

"White."

"That's the best," said Myra.

"Hush," he said, "it's still there."

But Myra knew her moment to strike, and she replied softly, "Now, am I making it up?"

Mark, still trying to keep what he's got in his inner vision going, said, "No-o-o." No, she wasn't making it up; it was true.

Something was changing in Mark. Just like that—a change in consciousness.

USE YOUR CREATIVE ABILITIES

Use your creative abilities to go a step further. Experiment with the spiritual exercises, and try new things. You're in your own God Worlds. I've gone to different extremes, trying very complicated exercises I developed for myself, dropping them when they didn't work anymore.

It's like a vein of gold running through a mountain. You're on it for awhile, then the vein runs out and you have to scout around and find another one.

Are you learning something new every day from what you're doing? Are you getting insight and help from within? This is what you ought to be working for.

You can try any of the following spiritual exercises to help you get started.

A SIMPLE SPIRITUAL EXERCISE TO TRY

Try this simple spiritual exercise to help you hear and see the two aspects of God, the Light and Sound.

Try this simple spiritual exercise to help you hear and see the two aspects of God, the Light and Sound.

Go somewhere quiet. Sit or lie down in a comfortable place. Put your attention on your Spiritual Eye: a point just above and behind your eyebrows. With eyes lightly shut, begin to sing a holy word or phrase, such as *HU, God, Holy Spirit,* or *Show me thy ways, O Lord.* But fill your heart with love before you approach the altar of God, because only the pure may come.

Be patient. Do this exercise daily for several weeks, for a limit of twenty minutes each time. Sit, sing, and wait. God speaks only when you are able to listen.

There is more to the pursuit of God than luck.

Be patient. Sit, sing, and wait. God speaks only when you are able to listen.

Monkeys of the Mind Technique

When your mind jumps around, you can visualize your thoughts as monkeys jumping around. See what you can do to make them calm down instead of being mischievous. You're working with an imaginative technique here, which gives you a multitude of possibilities.

Visualize a door that you want to walk through, but you can't because the monkeys are jumping all around in front of it. Say to yourself, I've got to get the monkeys quieted down, and then I can go through the door and enter into the worlds of Light and Sound.

Give the monkeys bright, attractive little toys with bells, or feed them bananas. You can get so involved in quieting the monkeys of the mind that you'll find you're enjoying yourself.

Soul is now expressing Itself.

As soon as you get them settled down, make a dash for the door. On the other side is the pure golden Light of God.

The monkeys of the mind are merely the guardians of the door. They'll do everything possible to keep you from going through. Once you figure out a way to calm them down, then you're ready to go beyond into the inner worlds.

OPEN-EYED EXERCISE: CONTEMPLATION IS APPRECIATION

Another word for contemplation is *appreciation*. Think about all the reasons you have to be grateful.

True contemplation is reflecting on the blessings of God in your life.

Think about the gifts in your life that have come from God, from the Holy Spirit, that make this life worth living. Think about the adventures that are coming, and be grateful for the strength to meet tomorrow.

Appreciate the gift of life.

True contemplation is reflecting on the blessings of God in your life. It's not complex, there are many ways to do it, and it certainly will enrich you.

A SPIRITUAL EXERCISE TO COMBINE CONTEMPLATION AND DREAMS

A simple method of moving into the higher states of awareness is to combine contemplation and dreams. Find a quiet place for contemplation.

For a period of fifteen or twenty minutes a day, shut your eyes and put attention upon your Spiritual Eye. This is the spiritual organ of inner vision. It sits between the eyebrows, about an inch and a half in.

Look gently at an imaginary screen between the eyebrows and softly begin to sing *Jesus, God, HU,* or *Mahanta. Wah Z** is also acceptable.

Look for a Blue Light upon the inner screen. This is the Light of God. There may not be this Light, but you may hear a Sound. The Sound is the other manifestation of the ECK, or Holy Spirit. It can be almost any sound of nature or musical instrument that you can imagine. The Light and Sound, when they appear, are assurance of your contact with the Word of God.

The second part of this exercise is for the dream state. Prepare for sleep by singing one of the words

Your Spiritual Eye is the spiritual organ of inner vision. Look for a Blue Light upon the inner screen. This is the Light of God.

---

*The spiritual name of Sri Harold Klemp, the Mahanta, the Living ECK Master—spiritual leader of Eckankar and inner guide for those who follow Eckankar.

given above. This is to set into motion an affinity with the Sound Current, the Holy Spirit. For a few minutes, sing the word you have chosen. When you are ready for sleep, imagine that you are walking in a park or watching a quiet sunset with someone you love. A loved one can open our heart and dispel any fear. Love is necessary if one is to enter the awakened dream state.

To set into motion an affinity with the Sound Current, the Holy Spirit, sing the word you have chosen.

Finally, keep a diary of whatever comes to mind in contemplation or during your dream state. A mutual confidence will develop between your inner and outer selves, and the two techniques above will help accomplish that.

This is a good way to start the dream teachings of ECK.

7

A GUIDE TO THE MOST SECRET PART OF YOURSELF

The most secret part of yourself is the heart of love. The greatest gift life can give you is a means to come into contact with this mysterious part, which is the secret to life itself.

Seekers in ages past discovered and followed a teacher who could guide them beyond the spiritual limitations of body and mind. Countless others, including many saints, have mastered the art and science of Soul Travel.

In Eckankar, an earnest seeker is under the protection of a spiritual guide known as the Mahanta. This is the Spiritual Traveler. As the Mahanta he is the Inner Master, the one who comes on the other planes to impart knowledge, truth, and wisdom.

The Mahanta is a state of consciousness. It is a spiritual state of consciousness very much like the Buddha consciousness or the Christ consciousness. The Living ECK Master is the other half of the title *the Mahanta, the Living ECK Master.* This means the outer spiritual teacher, myself.

The teachings of Eckankar speak very directly and very distinctly of the two parts of the Master: the Inner Master and the Outer Master. The Inner Master is the Mahanta, and the Outer Master is the Living ECK Master.

The Inner Master is not a physical being. It is someone you see in the inner planes during contemplation or in the dream state. He may look like me, he may look like another ECK Master, or he may even look the same as Christ. All it is, really, is the merging of the Light and Sound of God into a matrix, into a form which appears as a person. This, then, becomes the inner guide which steers a person through the pitfalls of karma, the troubles we make for ourselves through ignorance of the spiritual laws.

The merging of the Light and Sound of God into a matrix becomes the inner guide which steers a person through the pitfalls of karma, the troubles we make for ourselves through ignorance of the spiritual laws.

The Master often works in the dream state because it is easier to get through. Fears can inhibit and prevent one from exercising the freedom and power and wisdom which are the birthright of Soul. In the dream state, the Inner Master can begin working with you to familiarize and make you comfortable with what comes on the other side.

You can get to the most secret part of yourself through contemplation, through the Spiritual Exercises of ECK. Contemplation is a conversation with the most secret, most genuine, and most mysterious part of yourself.

THE HAND OF GOD SAVED HER LIFE

"Claudia" is from Tennessee. She was involved in a serious car accident. But before I tell this story, I need to point out her routine. I mention this because it's something for you to take to heart and realize how important it is to imbue yourself with the living essence of the Light and Sound of God.

Every morning, first thing, Claudia does a contemplation. When she finishes, she gets ready for work. When she gets into her car, the first thing she does is declare herself a clear channel for God, the Holy Spirit, and the Mahanta. In the ECK parlance this is the Sugmad, the ECK, and the Mahanta. And then she sets out on the road with her CD of the HU song playing in the car. She sings HU with all her might as she drives the forty minutes to work.

One day as Claudia drove along the freeway, the traffic screeched to a halt in front of her. She hit the brakes, came to a safe stop, and looked in the rearview mirror. She realized the semitruck behind her would be unable to stop. She also realized her seat belt was unbuckled and there was no time to fasten it. She screamed, "God, please help me!"

At that moment she felt a giant hand of God surround her, holding her gently in its grip. She knew this as the hand of the Mahanta.

The truck hit the back of her Toyota Camry, a brand-new car, and pushed the trunk all the way up to the rear seats. The car was pushed into the car ahead of hers, crunching the engine back up to the dashboard. But through it all, her CD player kept playing the HU song. And there sat Claudia.

The Mahanta had lifted her out of the body, and when she returned, a fireman was holding her hand. He was the first on the scene.

How important it is to imbue yourself with the living essence of the Light and Sound of God. Every morning, first thing, Claudia does a contemplation.

So the firefighter said, "Hold on, ma'am, an ambulance is on the way." Claudia was very calm and detached. She looked at him and said, "I'm not hurt. I'm OK." And he said, "Have you looked at your car?" She said, "Of course not. I haven't been able to get out of this seat." He said, "Well, let me tell you about the car."

Basically, it looked like an accordion. Right in the middle of it all sat Claudia. When the ambulance came, they insisted she go to the hospital because they were sure there would be internal injuries.

She arrived at the hospital. The doctor did a whole battery of X-rays. No broken bones, no scratches, no bruises. So the doctor gave her a handful of pills. He said, "You're going to need these tomorrow because you're going to be in a world of hurt." And she said, "No, I won't." She went home.

Claudia realized that the Mahanta was the hand of God that had saved her life.

Next morning Claudia woke up without any pain. She threw the pills away, and that was the end of that. And she realized that the Mahanta was the hand of God that had saved her life.

DOOR OF SOUL SPIRITUAL EXERCISE

The door of Soul opens inward. No amount of pushing on the wrong side will open it. For this reason, twenty minutes to half an hour is the limit to spend on a spiritual exercise during a session unless an experience has begun. Then, of course, see it through to the end.

To have an experience with the Light and Sound of God or the Inner Master, use this two-part technique:

1. In contemplation sometime during the day, count backward slowly from ten to one. Then try to see yourself standing beside your human self, which is at rest. Keep this part to half an hour or less.

2. The second part of this technique comes at night when you are preparing for sleep. Speak to the Dream Master, the Mahanta. Say to him, "I give you permission to lead me into the Far Country,* to the right places and people."

Now go to sleep. Give no further thought to this technique. Your permission to the Mahanta unlocks the unconscious mind and gives the human mind a chance to retain a memory of your dream travels come morning.

That's all there is to this two-part dream exercise.

Be sure a dream notebook is within easy reach. Keep notes. Remember that in the spiritual field,

Speak to the Dream Master, the Mahanta. Say to him, "I give you permission to lead me into the Far Country, to the right places and people."

---

*The vast world lying beyond the earth plane; a series of spiritual universes which can be experienced by Soul.

there is no need to push things. With ECK in your life, the gifts of Spirit, like love and wisdom, will now start coming to your attention.

8

SOUL TRAVEL WITH THE SPIRITUAL EXERCISES OF ECK

*S*oul Travel is a valuable skill that can be learned by almost anyone who is willing to invest the time and patience. It is a bridge over the gulf that divides the human from the spiritual consciousness.

Soul Travel is a natural progression that is reached through the Spiritual Exercises of ECK.

A chela in Africa lay down in bed, covered his ears with pillows, and listened to the ECK Sound, which was like a sibilant, rushing wind in the distance—but still very close and within him. Soon, he felt a sucking motion at the top of his head, but he was not afraid. He then felt himself totally withdraw from his physical body and hover in space over the bed.

"The whole of this space was lighted with shimmering atoms and bright giant and small stars," he said. He looked at himself and discovered he was in the radiant Soul body, very youthful and full of energy and power.

Then he sang "Sugmad," a name for God, in a gentle lullaby. In that moment he realized that all the atoms and all the stars were part of him. As he sang quietly to himself, an energy vibrated continuously and flowed out from him to sustain all things

He looked at himself and discovered he was in the radiant Soul body, very youthful and full of energy and power.

and beings in this unending universe of stars. He felt mercy and love for all beings in this universe of light. He experienced a great Sound flowing from his center, touching and giving joyful bliss, life, and power to all in his universe. This left him in spiritual ecstasy, because of the act of giving.

The ecstasy returns to him even now in his physical state. This was an experience of brief homage paid to the Sugmad (God), and it has enhanced his life in every way.

This experience began as Soul Travel, but it went beyond that and ended as a spiritual journey to God.

This experience began as Soul Travel, but it went beyond that and ended as a spiritual journey to God. A touch of God is not the Sugmad in Its fullness, because the God experience, all at once, would devastate the individual, causing a setback for many ages.

The classic Soul Travel experience is leaving the human body in full awareness and having the Light and Sound of God flow directly into the Soul body. But some people have done that in earlier incarnations and have no desire to go through the ABCs of spiritual school again. The Mahanta may give them a few brief refresher Soul Travel experiences, and from then on they go on to seeing, knowing, and being. This phase of experience in ECK is the ECKshar consciousness. To see, know, and be are the qualities of Soul that are at the forefront of attention in the Soul Plane and above.

Beginners in Soul Travel usually stay close to the body. The Mahanta or his designee will help the individual get above the human state of consciousness and take a short journey in the near Astral Plane. These experiences may include the awareness of moving out of the body, going through ceilings or walls, and flying into a blackness. A patch of light glimmers at the edge of the blackness, and the novice Soul Traveler emerges into the light, which is a world of light.

Here he may walk city streets that closely resemble those on earth. The people, however, are busy with duties that are unknown on earth: welcoming new arrivals who have died on the Physical Plane and are ready to resume their lives on the Astral, guiding people who have come to the Astral Plane by chance during a dream, and serving the spiritual hierarchy in many other things that are routinely done to make life go on in the worlds of God.

Soul Travel is a means of hearing the Sound and seeing the Light of God, in a way which cannot be done in the human body. The Sound and Light are the wave upon which Soul rides back into the kingdom of heaven; they are the twin aspects of ECK. When an individual has gone through the phases of visions, dreams, Soul Travel, and the ECKshar consciousness, and is an experienced traveler in all the regions of God, then he receives the enlightenment of God. This is God Consciousness, and nothing more can be said about it here because words fail.

The Sound and Light are the wave upon which Soul rides back into the kingdom of heaven; they are the twin aspects of ECK.

A SPIRITUAL EXERCISE TO TRAIN THE IMAGINATION

The imaginative faculty within yourself is like a muscle. You're going to have to train it day after day. What you are actually doing is learning how to become aware and observant of yourself in a different state of consciousness.

One way is to go to different places in your imagination. Maybe you'll want to re-create a plane ride: I'm sitting in the airplane seat. What do I see? What do the people look like? What happens when I walk down the aisle? What is on the food tray?

As you go through the day, you'll find yourself looking at objects and making mental notes, because that physical information about the dresser or the clothes in your closet will be helpful when you sit down in your chair and try to visualize it for Soul Travel.

As dramatic as classic Soul Travel experiences are, it is just as exciting to recognize the presence of God's love in your everyday life.

THE POWER OF LOVE

As dramatic as classic Soul Travel experiences are, it is just as exciting to recognize the presence of God's love in your everyday life. This expanded awareness is another benefit of Soul Travel and the Spiritual Exercises of ECK.

A woman I'll call Ann was having a difficult time

with her husband, whom I'll call Thomas. He did not like the fact that Ann followed the practices of Eckankar, which, of course, included the Spiritual Exercises of ECK. So anytime she tried to do the spiritual exercises, he would come in and disturb her. She would sometimes go to a far corner of their home, or she'd try it at different times of the day. But their schedules were such that they were home together most of the time. And Thomas would always interrupt her.

Ann, however, was patient. She never said anything, but she often wondered, *What can I do to help him understand the beauty and the treasure I've found in the teachings of ECK? How can I ever get him to understand this?*

She asked the Mahanta, the Inner Master, "What can I do to help my husband understand why I love the ECK?"

Ann went to an Eckankar seminar, and while there she attended a workshop titled "Recognizing God's Presence in Your Everyday Life."

At the workshop she began to share experiences from her own life. Apparently the audience enjoyed it, because they were laughing. Warm, encouraging, supporting laughter. She felt like she belonged. These people understood.

At the end of the workshop, she had the answer to her question of how to talk to her husband about ECK. She realized she could talk about the coincidences that occur. *That* she could do.

She asked the Mahanta, the Inner Master, "What can I do to help my husband understand why I love the ECK?"

During the whole weekend, she had been look-ing for some little gift for him, because she loves Thomas very dearly. But she couldn't find anything until it was time to leave for home. Then, following an inner nudge, she found herself in a hotel lobby. Ann stood there wondering, *Well, why did that inner nudge tell me to come here?* Then she saw a light com-ing from around a corner. It belonged to a little shop which was still open. Up on a shelf, she saw some old CDs. She looked through them, and there was an album by The Platters from the 1950s. They were a very popular singing group back then. Ann had only five dollars and some change in cash, so she knew the gift could not be a very expensive one. And guess what—the CD was five dollars plus tax. So she bought it, put it in her luggage, and flew home.

Ann stood there wonder-ing, Well, why did that inner nudge tell me to come here?

Thomas picked her up at the airport. On their way home, he told her about something very impor-tant and heartwarming that had happened to him. He has an act in a club, and during one of his perfor-mances, there was a surprise guest. The man had come to the club to enjoy dinner and a show, and after-ward he made himself known to Thomas. It turned out to be someone Thomas had performed with many years ago. This man had gone on to join the singing group The Platters.

Ann didn't have a chance to tell him about the gift because his story took the whole ride home. When they got inside, she reached in her bag, pulled out the CD, and gave it to him.

Thomas just stood there, his eyes wide open and his mouth hanging open too.

As she began to laugh, he said, "It's this thing between us."

"It's what I call the work of the Holy Spirit, the ECK," she said. "This is more than a coincidence. You can see that. The ECK did this for a reason." And suddenly Thomas had an insight into what this path she practiced was all about.

After that, Thomas was much more open about her practicing the Spiritual Exercises of ECK. And at last report, he disturbed her much less than he had before.

Well, such is the power of love. Love on both sides—Ann's love for her husband, and his love for her.

Such is the power of love. Love on both sides—Ann's love for her husband, and his love for her.

I Know Where It Is!

"Fred" tells of an experience that convinced him there was something to Eckankar, HU, Soul Travel, and maybe even the Spiritual Eye, although he wasn't a member of Eckankar.

Fred and his wife, whom I'll call Paula, live in Canada. Paula originally came from Germany, and after they'd become settled in Canada, they went back to Germany to get her belongings.

When they were ready to start packing up her things, Paula said, "You take care of everything in the office and mark the boxes Office. Take care of the files and whatever else you find in there."

So Fred went to it and put everything in boxes. In a short while, there were rows and rows of boxes stacked to the ceiling. After they'd been at this a day or so, Paula said, "Oh, by the way, did you happen to see this certain file?" She described the file and said she needed it.

Fred said, "No, I don't know anything about the files. You just said pack them; I didn't read them."

But Paula insisted, "We're just going to have to find it."

All these Office boxes were mixed in with the rest of the boxes. So as they had time, they pulled boxes down and looked for the file. This went on until the night before the moving company came to pick up the boxes. At this point Paula said, "I know how we can find it."

Paula said, "I know how we can find it. We'll do a contemplation."

"What?" he said. By then it was late at night, and poor Fred was so tired.

Paula said, "Come in here to the couch. We'll sit down and do a contemplation."

"What?" he said again. Paula hadn't talked to him too much about contemplation or anything.

"We'll sing HU," she said.

Fred had heard about HU, the holy name for God, just one time before. But he was too tired to argue. So he sat down on the couch with his wife, and she said, "Put your attention at the Spiritual Eye, which is just a little above and behind your eyebrows."

They sang HU, and Fred felt a slight pressure up there. Then suddenly, just as clearly as a slide projector throwing a picture up on a white screen, he saw the box. He saw the row, and he saw where it was in the row. They came out of contemplation, and he said to Paula, "I know where the box is."

They went into the room, and Fred located the box in the second row, third box back from the wall, at a certain height. Paula started digging into that box, and Fred said, "You'll find that the file is upside-down in the box. That's why we couldn't find it before."

Paula found a file that was upside-down. She pulled it out, and it was the very file they had been looking for all that time. They were both astounded.

Fred's first thought was, *Well, maybe this was just partly something in my subconscious mind.* "That's where it was, dear; it was in my subconscious mind," he said.

"But you didn't open the file," said Paula. "You didn't even know what it was."

"That's right. You're right, dear," said Fred.

After all, what's a husband to say?

But he got to thinking, *You know, she's told me about Soul Travel and Eckankar, and maybe there's just something to it.*

They sang HU. Then they came out of contemplation, and he said to Paula, "I know where the box is."

MAY I SEE THE FACE OF GOD?

I'd like to tell you about Kristy. Kristy has written to me many times in the past and has often mentioned Misha, her beautiful Siamese cat.

He's got this quiet way of walking; he's like a ghost, moving very quietly. Kristy will be working at her desk; then the next moment, right on the sofa next to her, there's Misha. Kristy never hears him come. He'll appear in the kitchen; suddenly, there's Misha, just to be near her. He's a very dignified cat, very stately. He has these piercing, penetrating, loving eyes.

One day, Kristy was going to do a spiritual exercise. She sat down, and this one question came. It had been through her mind a couple of times before, and she had always forgotten about it. But this time it came: "May I see the face of God?"

She dared to ask the Inner Master, "May I see the face of God?"

So this time, in contemplation, she dared to ask the Inner Master, "May I see the face of God?" She had the courage to ask.

Kristy sat there quietly, listening for anything, looking on her inner screen. Looking, listening. Then she heard this funny little sound. She listened, and it wasn't a sound from the inner planes. It was some sound out here. *Strange,* she thought. *I've never heard that peculiar sound before. What could it be? It couldn't be Misha. Misha walks like a ghost. I never hear Misha walking anywhere. Misha just appears.*

So Kristy focused her attention, got rid of all those little thoughts that try to take a person's attention away from the Third Eye—that little place back by the pineal gland in the middle of the head. She looked there, her eyes shut, and crowded out all these outside noises and distractions. She heard that sound again. She wondered, *Shall I peek?*

She opened her eyes, and seated right in front of her, looking right into her eyes, was Misha. He was just looking at her: wise, eternal, and so full of love. Kristy looked at him and thought, *If ever there was a huge symbol of love, it's Misha. And what is God? God is love. So in answer to my question,* May I see the face of God? *I hear this little sound; Misha makes this little sound he's never made before. I open my eyes and realize then that the love of God is all around me, as near and dear as Misha.*

So Kristy laughed and laughed, because it was like a divine joke to teach her the truth—to help her through the illusion of "Where is this face of God?"

Kristy saw truth. It's all around you. The Light of God is in every person. Enjoy the good in others. Overlook and forgive the negative where Soul still needs to polish.

Kristy saw truth. It's all around you. The Light of God is in every person.

AN ADVANCED SPIRITUAL EXERCISE TO EXPLORE THE LEVELS OF HEAVEN

A spiritual exercise that will be of help in the dream state and also with Soul Travel is called the

Formula technique. It can help you reach any level from the Second to Fifth planes.

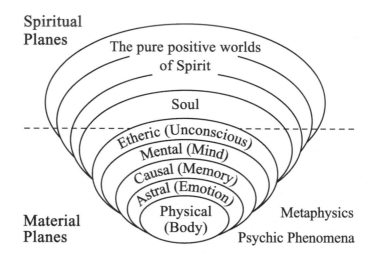

The God Worlds of ECK

You may want to go to the second level, the Astral Plane, which corresponds to the emotional body, to find out why there is an emotional bond with another person.

The third level, the Causal Plane, is where you find the seed of all karma created in the past and learn about the past lives that influence you today.

The Mental Plane is the level where mental processes originate, where inspiration and ideas may be found in whatever field you are interested in. At the top of this fourth level is the Etheric Plane, which corresponds to the subconscious or unconscious attitudes that motivate you.

The Causal Plane is where you find the seed of all karma and learn about the past lives that influence you today.

Then comes the Soul Plane, the level of Self-Realization, the first of the true spiritual worlds.

Sometimes you may have an experience on the inner planes and wonder whether it happened on the Astral, Causal, or Mental Plane.

It can be tricky to distinguish the difference. Many of the experiences on the Mental Plane and the Astral Plane, for instance, are similar enough that sometimes you can't tell on which plane they occurred. It would be nice if someone held up a brightly painted sign in the dream state: "You have arrived on the Astral Plane!" But you can't count on it.

The Formula technique is like a visitor's pass to the other planes. It can even be used by a First or Second Initiate to visit the Soul Plane.

This spiritual exercise, which takes about fifteen to twenty minutes, is done at bedtime. It's very simple, and it goes with the sound of HU, a holy name for God.

To reach the Second, or Astral, Plane, use Formula Two. First chant HU two times, then breathe deeply two times. Repeat it again—chant HU twice and breathe deeply twice. Then do it again—HU two times, breathe two times.

You don't have to set your timer, because all of a sudden you will know that it's time to stop chanting and go to sleep. If you do the spiritual exercise lying on your back, just roll over, make yourself comfortable, and very gently hold the thought *Formula Two* in mind as you drift off to sleep.

The Formula technique is like a visitor's pass to the other planes.

Going to the Third, or Causal, Plane, the plane of seed karma and past lives, is equally simple with Formula Three: Chant HU three times and breathe deeply three times. Repeat it again—three HUs, three breaths. Keep doing this until you know within that it's time to quit. As you go to sleep, very gently, without becoming locked on it, try to hold the thought *Formula Three*.

You can aim for the Mental Plane by chanting four HUs, taking four deep breaths, and falling asleep with *Formula Four* lightly in mind.

To visit the Soul Plane, chant HU five times, breathe five times, and gently think, *Formula Five*.

If you wake up and remember something that happened on the inner planes, try to write it down right then.

If you wake up and remember something that happened on the inner planes, try to write it down right then, because you'll probably forget most of it by morning.

When writing the experiences in your dream journal, you will find it helpful to write at the top of the page which formula you used, to help you remember what you were trying to achieve that night. Then add the date, and write down the experience. Eventually you will develop a feel for which plane you should be working on that particular evening.

Once you have any degree of success with this Formula technique, you will start to see a different texture to the experiences on each plane. Try to see if there is a thread that runs through them. In one way or another, Soul will try to come through to give you what you need to know for your spiritual unfoldment.

Writing these experiences down as they come is a most difficult discipline. But if you can get in the habit, you will find the full spectrum of your life slowly opening to you, like the petals of a flower.

You will find your life slowly opening to you.

9

WHAT IS
SPIRITUAL FREEDOM?

*T*he ultimate state of spiritual freedom brings wisdom, love, and spiritual power. But there are stages in between. We expand or unfold from no freedom into a greater state of spiritual freedom.

One morning I went into the bathroom, and there was a huge spider, a daddy longlegs, on my bath towel. I'd seen him under a shelf a week before, and as long as he stayed there, I didn't care. But it might be hard on him to be on my towel; he might get crunched, or we might both have a fright when I tried to dry myself.

So I went downstairs and got a glass and an index card. It wasn't even a struggle getting him into the glass. I carried him to the garage and balanced the glass in one hand as I reached to push the button for the garage-door opener.

As I pressed the button, there was an enormous blue flash. It startled me so much I almost dropped the glass. The spider fell to the floor and scurried away.

SEEING PAST ILLUSION

Whenever something very startling like this happens, I know there's a spiritual lesson in it. It looked like the light had burned out on the garage-door opener.

The ultimate state of spiritual freedom brings wisdom, love, and spiritual power. But there are stages in between.

"As long as I'm here, I'll replace that burned-out lightbulb," I said to my wife. So I went back inside to get a new bulb.

I came back out, stood on a stepladder, and screwed in the bulb. It stayed lit for about five seconds, then went out.

"Oh no," I said, "we've got big problems." It looked like there was a short in the garage-door opener. "Now the door's going to be frozen in the open position, and anyone can come in and steal my lawn mower or snow thrower," I told my wife. *Maybe this isn't so bad*, I thought.

After thinking about this problem and how I was going to fix it, it occurred to me to try the garage-door opener again. A little skeptical, I walked over to the button and pressed it.

To my surprise, the light came on immediately, and the door closed.

I realized our garage-door opener has a ten-minute timer. The light comes on when the door opens, then it shuts off after ten minutes. Apparently by the time I went inside and found a new bulb, nine minutes and fifty-five seconds had passed.

Sometimes forces of illusion try to make us see things through a cloud.

It was interesting timing. I would have drawn the wrong conclusion; I did for a few seconds. But when it happened so suddenly, I asked, "What else could be wrong?"

Sometimes forces of illusion try to make us see things through a cloud.

We draw the wrong conclusions, like I did when I thought the garage-door opener was broken. But because I listened to the inner nudge to try once more, the illusion was broken instead.

A frozen garage door on a Sunday morning right before you leave the house could be a problem, unless you don't care too much about mowing the lawn or clearing snow from the driveway in winter. My wife wouldn't have minded, actually. She doesn't want me to mow the lawn or do these things.

We hear about how we should have an easy life, not have too much tension. But under certain conditions, challenge is good. Maybe we live longer. There are studies done that show people who live alone live a shorter time than people who have someone else in the home. I think the constant presence of someone else's opinion about how you should live your life has staying power.

It's good to live longer if we are still working on achieving the steps toward spiritual freedom. That way we can learn the lessons that we would otherwise not get in this lifetime.

What is spiritual freedom?

Spiritual freedom is when a responsibility is removed and gives us more time to do the things we really want to do or like to do that are of a spiritual direction. In everyday terms, it's similar to what parents feel when the last teenager leaves home. Or what the teenager feels when he or she gets a driver's license. It's a degree of spiritual freedom.

What is spiritual freedom? In everyday terms, it's similar to what parents feel when the last teenager leaves home.

LEAVING THE NEST

When my daughter graduated from high school, I said, "Thank God."

If you're a parent, you can understand what I mean. If the child doesn't graduate, it's like a baby robin who doesn't leave the nest. By the end of summer, the parent robins get pretty thin from chasing around getting food for their young. Parents can run themselves ragged for their fledglings.

In a healthy family when the children are finally ready to leave home, the parents say, "Sure, we'll lend you some money to leave. Don't forget to write. And remember that eighteen is the cutoff age for unlimited financial aid."

The thought of going back to life the way it was before you had children takes awhile to soak in sometimes. Just the thought of it can give you this feeling of lightness and happiness. Yet some parents are heartbroken, seeing the home suddenly empty. What are they going to fill their lives with now? Other parents, however, are happy to go out to dinner and not have to worry about being home before dark.

When this rite of passage occurs for the child, it's a state of freedom reached by the parents too.

RITE OF PASSAGE

When this rite of passage occurs for the child, it's a state of freedom reached by the parents too.

This is as it should be; it's basically what nature does. The only species that violates this is the human being, when grown children become professional beggars by hanging on at home. Any parent with any sense of humanity cannot throw them out, even though it might be the best thing to do for both parent and child.

What does life require of us? To be able to survive, to go out there and have the experiences of life, and to learn from them. To become better spiritual beings.

And by becoming better spiritual beings, we become more self-sufficient. We become better able to handle ourselves in one crisis after another, as well as in the good times. This moves us toward spiritual freedom in this lifetime.

When you have more spiritual freedom, you have more happiness and independence. This is what we are looking for.

When you have more spiritual freedom, you have more happiness and independence. This is what we are looking for.

One summer, my daughter went to Alaska to work in a fish cannery. I strongly encouraged her, short of buying the plane ticket, which I let her earn herself. She was also earning spending money; she wanted to have two or three hundred dollars by the time she left. She said her friends would be taking ninety or one hundred dollars each. "You're going to do fine," I told her.

But I think she decided to take it easy for a few weeks before she left. She was going with six friends, and they spent a week packing things into duffel bags.

Just before she left, I talked with her again on the phone. "How much money do you have?" I asked.

"About a hundred dollars," she said.

"What happened?" I asked. "You were going to have a lot more."

"Well, Dad," she said, "I had to pack."

I realized it doesn't take two weeks to pack a duffel bag, but I also wasn't going anywhere in this argument.

"Call me if you need any money," I told her.

I had told her to take this adventure because if she stayed home she'd regret it for the rest of her life. She and her friends got their courage from each other. It was enough to get them to Alaska. They're out on the first of the Aleutian Islands—no trees, no brush, just sand and three or four dormitories for the students who come to process the fish. She got homesick quickly. There's no radio, no TV.

GIVING OTHERS FREEDOM

After my daughter had left, her mother called me. "Moonies are running that cannery," she said. She was concerned. "What if they try to change her religion?"

"I don't care," I said. "If she wants to leave Eckankar and become a Moonie or a Lutheran or a Catholic or a Hindu or anything, it's OK. I don't own her." I had spent the better part of eighteen years imagining the worst thing this child could ever do to me. Because if you can figure that out, the child can't control you.

A dear friend of mine who grew up a Southern

I said, "If she wants to leave Eckankar and become a Moonie or a Lutheran or a Catholic or a Hindu or anything, it's OK. I don't own her."

Baptist raised two sons; one became a Mormon (and married one), and one became an atheist. My friend always let people enjoy their religious freedom, even at home.

WHEN LOVE REPLACES FEAR

What is spiritual freedom?

Spiritual freedom is growing into a state of more godliness. Becoming more aware of the presence of God.

How do you do this? By becoming aware of the lessons behind your everyday experiences. This is how you grow into a loving awareness of the presence of God.

Most people live under the hand of fear. You buy life insurance; you wear seat belts. Why? Because you're afraid of what might happen if you get into an accident.

When you get a little more spiritual freedom, love comes into your heart and replaces fear with wisdom. This is the golden heart. You start making decisions based on a greater degree of wisdom instead of fear. You say, "Maybe I'm not wearing this seat belt out of fear; I just find it a wise thing to do."

But how do you get your heart open?

Spiritual freedom is growing into a state of more godliness. By becoming aware of the lessons behind your everyday experiences, you grow into a loving awareness of the presence of God.

10

HOW TO FIND SPIRITUAL FREEDOM IN THIS LIFETIME

$\mathcal{L}$ife could not exist without either the Light and Sound of God. They show up in many different ways here in the material plane. They create the forms within which we move to get the spiritual experience we need to have spiritual freedom.

A GIFT OF LAUGHTER

A friend told me the story of "Helga" and "Sven," a Swedish couple who traveled to New York City. They were unsophisticated travelers, and when their friends learned where they were going, everyone warned them about crime in New York. "Don't ride the subway; watch out for cabdrivers," they said.

But the Swedish couple arrived safely, got to their hotel, and even went on a few guided tours. They had a few days free, but they didn't want to leave their hotel room because of all the terrible things that could happen out there.

One day they were running short of refreshments, and since room service was too expensive for their budget, Helga decided to take her life in her hands and go to the corner store. As she got on the elevator, a huge man came in with a huge dog. The man was the leader of a rock band; he had a huge head of hair, well-worn jeans, and chains around his neck.

Helga was petrified; she stood in the corner of the elevator shaking as the doors closed. All the warnings of her friends came back to her mind. And here her worst fears had walked right into the elevator with her.

The dog was curious about Helga and moved over to her. He began sniffing her dress, as dogs do.

"Down," the rock musician commanded.

The dog got down on the floor. And Helga got down right beside him, her hands over her head.

The rock musician began to laugh. He laughed until tears streamed down his face.

The rock musician began to laugh. He laughed until tears streamed down his face. He was still laughing as the elevator doors opened and he walked across the lobby into the street.

Poor Helga was so scared she got off the elevator on her hands and knees. Finally gathering her courage, she stood up and went to the corner store. When she got back to the hotel room, she was too embarrassed to tell Sven what had happened.

For the next few days, every time the couple went down to the hotel dining room, the whole rock band was there. As soon as Helga walked in, the entire group started to laugh. They laughed until tears ran down their faces and they finally had to leave the dining room. Sven wondered what had happened.

Mercifully, the day came when they could check out and return home to Europe, back to sanity. Helga and Sven went to the front desk to pay their large bill, but the clerk said, "Your bill's paid for. And here's a letter for the lady."

The letter was from the rock musician.

"Thank you so much," he had written. "I have never laughed so much in my whole life. But I realize we embarrassed you, and to make up for this I am paying for your hotel room. We wish you a happy journey. Thank you for the joy and laughter you brought to us."

This was the journey of the Swedish couple to New York City, where they learned that fear sometimes can be overcome by love. Because as the musician began to laugh, love came into his heart. It also came to the Swedish couple when he was able to give the gift of love back to the woman who had inadvertently opened his heart.

The Swedish couple learned that fear sometimes can be overcome by love. Because as the musician began to laugh, love came into his heart.

WHAT IS SPIRITUAL FREEDOM?

It's hard to say exactly what spiritual freedom is. At times it's easier to say what it is not.

Sometimes when a person sees tragedy, has troubles, or finds his or her faith shaken, it causes that person to ask, "Why does God allow this to happen?" If you ask yourself that question, you would be one who does not have spiritual freedom.

If you are a person having troubles in your everyday life, you might say, "Now what purpose could there be to my having this kind of a situation at work where this person is constantly on my case, causing trouble for me? What possible reason could there be?" A person who has to ask such a question does not have spiritual freedom.

Or say people blame us for something that someone else did, and we feel we have been a victim of injustice. We ask, "Why does something like that happen to me?" We really don't understand. This is another indication that a person does not have spiritual freedom.

In other words, any person who cannot understand what's happening in life does not have spiritual freedom.

How do we identify those who do have it? This is very hard for me to explain.

SEEING GOD'S HAND IN EVERYTHING

A person who realizes God's hand is in everything that occurs in that person's life is someone who has a degree of spiritual freedom.

The easiest way is simply to say that a person who realizes God's hand is in everything that occurs in that person's life is someone who has a degree of spiritual freedom.

If you look at people who are constantly unhappy, complaining, or criticizing, you'd have to say that they aren't anywhere near having spiritual freedom. Then you find sweet people—the ones that life throws everything negative at that it can—and these people are always up. They're happy. They've had all kinds of losses and troubles, but if you met them in the store or on the street, you'd never guess.

These are people who have a degree of spiritual freedom. They can see, to some degree, that whatever is happening to them is a part of the spiritual plan. It's a part of their spiritual unfoldment.

One Step Forward

You'll often hear people like this say, "I don't understand why this happened to me, but I know it's for the good. In some way, it's for the good."

This is a step.

It's a better, or higher, step than someone who falls into the dark night of Soul when things happen and asks, "Why did this happen to me? Is God a loving God, or is God not a loving God?"

The question is Where is spiritual freedom?

Most of us, if we had it, wouldn't recognize it. And if we don't recognize it, what good is it?

Stumbling Blocks or Stepping-Stones?

The ECK, or Holy Spirit, provides the bricks and mortar. I'm here to point them out to you, to say, "Those are the bricks, and there's the mortar." Most people don't recognize them.

And what are you going to do with them?

The Holy Spirit provides them, somebody points them out to you, but it's up to you whether you use them as stumbling blocks or as stepping-stones.

There's a trend today in society. A person will take the mortar and slop it on the ground where it hardens into big clumps. It has sharp edges, and the person trips on it but always says it's somebody else's fault. To me, this is such a waste of spiritual potential.

You'll hear people like this say, "I don't understand why this happened to me, but I know it's for the good. In some way. This is a step.

CREATIVE ABILITY IS SURVIVAL

What does it mean to be a spiritual being?

It means to employ the highest force of creativity that is possible among people. Creative power means figuring your way out of a situation once you get yourself into it. Because most of the time we find ourselves in trouble that we've made ourselves.

Someone with the golden heart is someone who lives in the presence of God, in the spirit of love.

The definition of someone with the golden heart is someone who lives in the presence of God, in the spirit of love.

That means you pay more attention to the needs of other people than to your own. It doesn't mean neglecting your own needs, of course; a person who is unable to take care of himself or herself certainly isn't going to be able to help anyone else.

Until you become a strong human being—able to survive under any and all conditions—you're never going to be able to help anyone else. In Eckankar, we want to see people develop into strong human beings. This is a path for the strong. The meek shall inherit the earth, but the strong shall go into the highest reaches of heaven.

LOVE IN EXPRESSION

One of the tour guides at the Temple of ECK was asked a question by a visitor: "Can you explain this Light and Sound of God in one sentence?"

No one had ever asked her to do this. She was at a loss, but she did the best she could in two or three sentences. After that she was a little nervous that someone would ask her such a question again. She wondered how to answer it.

One day she was showing someone a framed quilt downstairs in the Temple. It had a large golden Ⓔ in the center. She spoke about love as the creative force. Love is the force that opens your heart and allows you to experience life in fuller measure than before. It allows you to have more joy and appreciation for life every day.

That evening she was home hanging a picture on her wall. As she stood back to admire how nice it looked, a message came to her from the Inner Master that answered her question.

"The Light and Sound is love in expression," he said.

Love is the doorway to spiritual freedom. And the Light and Sound of God opens that doorway of love. You must go through that doorway. You must have the love of God transform your life before you can realize the gift of spiritual freedom.

Love is the force that opens your heart and allows you to have more joy and appreciation for life every day.

The Wonder of You

Who could be more wonderful than you? You have, oh, so many blessings. All you need to do is recognize them.

Can you? Will you? Do you?

Look around. You live in a garden. Someone loved you so much that here you are, in a garden.

There is spiritual food all around, there to feed and nourish. All you need to do is get it.

You are one of the special people. Somehow you've become awake and opened your eyes. Now awake, you know you are special. You know you live in a very special garden, a garden of love. Someone loved you so much that you are here, and awake. What a blessing to know you are blessed.

So how'd you come to be? How'd you get here? Why? And where to next?

Questions in the midst of plenty. Thinking, thinking. Why, why? And, why, why?

All this and more is you, a so-wonderful you.

Handmade in heaven.

Cared for on earth.

And all you have to do is accept it, and you will recognize the wonder of you too.

You are Soul. Special. One of a kind. So love yourself, love God, and love others. That's what your stay in this place is to help you learn.

Set your sights high. Set them very high. Why not set your sights on God? God loves you and has from Its creation of you. You're handmade in heaven, by the Maker of life, love, freedom, and happiness too. Be happy, be you, just BE!

Put away your fear. Put away your doubt. And remember to put away your worry.

You are Soul. Special. One of a kind. So love yourself, love God, and love others. That's what your stay in this place is to help you learn. So look around and say thank you for all the blessings. Be grateful. Make sure this is a fruitful life. After all, why be here if you won't?

Such is the wonder of you. Wake up and sing! Glory in this garden of love, because the holy foods are all around. The best is yet to come.

Now let's leave creation and being from beyond the stars and return to the world of being that we've created. We've made our world and all that's in it. Slowly and surely we see that it is so.

Our realization of it has a starting point, a place where Soul's awakening begins in earnest.

A Special Reason for This Life

Odd as it may seem, you had a special reason for coming into this lifetime. It was to become a more godlike being, but most people do not realize this fact. They assume that birth is a fancy of destiny.

All the lives you have ever lived were for the polishing of Soul. You are now at a higher and more spiritual level than in any prior incarnation.

All the lives you have ever lived were for the polishing of Soul. Like it or not, you are now at a higher and more spiritual level than in any prior incarnation. So look at yourself. Do you like what you see? Keep in mind, whatever it is, for better or worse, it's of your own making.

You are the sum of all your thoughts, feelings, and actions from this life and every lifetime in the past.

People, in general, think of karma as an unpleasant force and less often as having a beneficial side. Take for example Mozart, already composing music at age five.

The rule of karma determines factors like male or female body, eye-hand coordination, long- or short-term memory retention, and desires. In addition, our karmic package includes race, ancestry, family, friends, economic and social standing, and much more besides.

However, what comes of those conditions depends upon the exercise of our free will.

The Law of Cause and Effect, or the Law of Karma, is always in play your whole life. You must know how to live in harmony with its exacting terms. The experiences that derive from an adolescent or mature understanding of that law will, in time, bring you to an acceptance of divine love. That's the reason you're here.

The Easy Way *discourses are a portal for you to enter the secret worlds that exist beyond our cosmos.*

SOUL'S AWAKENING—THE EASY WAY

The *Easy Way* discourses are a portal for you to enter the secret worlds that exist beyond our cosmos, the higher regions so well known to the ECK travelers and the saints of old.

Sarah became a member of Eckankar and received *The Easy Way Discourses*. One night, she had a dream. She found herself with the Mahanta—this is the Inner Master, the inner form of myself. They were with a group of people—strangers, but they weren't strangers.

The dream took place in a room that was beyond the definition of time or space. And in this room was a big book, just a single book. The group of people stood around it, and each in turn would flip to one page or another and pick out a word. Each person got a word.

Sarah found a word, but she hadn't been in ECK long enough to know what the word meant. The word was *Wah Z*. For some reason, she liked the word. She'd never heard it before. She hadn't come to it in the inner teachings, the more advanced teachings, and she hadn't run across it in any of the outer writings. She didn't realize that Wah Z, or sometimes Z for short, is the name of the Inner Master.

Sarah convinced all the people in this group on the inner planes to chant this word with her. So they all chanted Wah Z. She liked the sound of it.

Suddenly a light came into the room, a warm, bright light that reached into the very depths of her heart. It made her feel warm and full of love. As the experience was going on, someone walked into the room where she was sleeping and turned on the bedroom light.

It woke her, and she lost the experience. She was very upset by this, but she tried not to show it.

What she didn't realize is that that person didn't accidentally walk into the room and turn on the light. The ECK—or the Mahanta—arranged for the person to come in just at the highlight of the inner experience. Otherwise Sarah would have forgotten her experience.

While she was writing this in her spiritual journal, it suddenly came to her that this was her First

While writing in her spiritual journal, it came to her this was her First Initiation in ECK. She had entered a larger room.

Initiation in ECK, as indeed it was. She had entered a larger room. The First Initiation in ECK usually comes during the first year of study of the ECK discourses, when one has made a commitment to the teachings of ECK.* The ECK discourses are written with a secret, internal rhythm that gradually unfolds your consciousness in a very precise and orderly manner.

A MOST HOLY MOMENT

An initiation is a most holy moment. An ECK initiation is simply a spiritual rite that brings you closer to ECK, the Holy Spirit. Not only does the person getting the initiation walk into the presence of the Divine Spirit, but also the Initiator. Both are standing in the circle of Divine Spirit more so than they do ordinarily. A lot of people just aren't aware of it. But during the time of initiation, people open their awareness and recognize the linkup with Divine Spirit.

Little by little, your Spiritual Eye opens and your heart opens to love.

Sometimes the awareness of this linkup comes in a gentle way, like a dream. Sometimes it comes later, when you wake up one morning with a feeling of love and wholeness you've never felt before. It begins to change you in little ways. Little by little, your Spiritual Eye opens and your heart opens to love.

Your heart opens to love because the teachings of ECK are about receiving God's love. When you

*See Next Steps in Spiritual Exploration, pp. 107–112.

begin receiving God's love, that is the way to spiritual freedom.

How Soul May Come to the Launching Pad

The ECK initiations (particularly the Second Initiation) are the launching pad. Let's see how Soul may come to it. And what then? Let's also look at two recent members of Eckankar, a First and a Second Initiate.

"Lucia" is a First Initiate. She's been in Eckankar less than a year.

Before one can begin the big spiritual awakening, he must find the teachings of ECK. A friend introduced her to them when she was at a university in 1992. This was in the British West Indies. She received an Eckankar brochure and also learned that those wishing to receive truth must be willing to share the modest cost it takes to provide it. This calls for self-responsibility. It came as a shock to Lucia, however. So she did not become a member.

She nevertheless began to do the spiritual exercise of singing HU, our love song to God, given in the brochure. Her experiences with the Light and Sound of God began at once. They continue still.

This had been her situation:

Lucia was a devout Roman Catholic all her life. But her spiritual hunger was growing, unsatisfied by her church. She felt there was more to the "Me"

The ECK initiations are the launching pad. Let's see how Soul may come to it. And what then?

she was. Where, oh where, could she find out about that?

Then, suddenly, there was Eckankar.

Her spiritual hunger had called for something to quiet the insistent longing in her to develop a personal and deep communion with God. This, she felt, would make sense of her existence.

Her spiritual hunger had called for something to quiet the insistent longing in her to develop a personal and deep communion with God.

The very night of the day she'd received the brochure, she had a dream. Three men greeted her.

"Welcome to ECK," they said.

It was a realistic dream, but she was cautious. "How am I to know this is real?" she asked.

In response, a large wave of water rushed through her nearby house, but disturbed nothing and hurt no one. Her house, though, was left clean and spotless. And with the housecleaning came a marvelous feeling of warmth and being cared for. It stayed with her a very long time.

Yet she didn't commit to Eckankar. It would be three years until she did. In the meantime, she learned about karma and how it worked. Also about not intruding into the thoughts and deeds of others. Yet it wasn't enough. Her spiritual hunger grew.

Suddenly, in 1995, she decided to return to her hometown, which had an ECK center. She became a true Hound of Heaven. She'd found the trail, the scent of truth was strong, and she would follow it to the very end. So Lucia read every book about Eckankar that came her way. She went to every HU

Chant or ECK seminar.

Sound and Light experiences were with her from the very beginning, like the yellow light. Sounds too, like the chiming of bells. And many, many meetings with the Mahanta, the Inner Master.

Now Lucia is more content and loves herself and others more. She's compelled to do loving things for others.

"Jim" is a new Second Initiate. Before and after he received the initiation, his life seemed to fall apart. Old things broke and needed replacing.

His car was one of them. One day, he left it by the roadside, a steaming, smoking piece of junk. He would need a new used car. But inspection showed all of them unfit to make a reliable commute from country to city. His wife said to check out a new/ used car dealer she'd found and look for a used one there.

So he went. It was a large dealership, with several entrances. The Mahanta (his inner guide) guided him to an "off-lot lot," where cars were sold that the dealer felt had better prospects there. Jim found his car.

Jim realized that his old car was him before the Second Initiation, the new one is him now. The old one had gone as far as it could. The new one can take him where he needs to go. He's learning.

Sound and Light experiences were with her from the very beginning, like the yellow light. Sounds too, like the chiming of bells. And meetings with the Mahanta, the Inner Master.

THE WAY TO SPIRITUAL FREEDOM

The way to spiritual freedom is really very easy. But first you've got to recognize that there is a need to have spiritual freedom. That's a big step. Most people never come to that in a single lifetime. It never occurs to them that they don't have spiritual freedom.

Once you come to the realization that you are without spiritual freedom, then comes the question of how you go about getting it.

In the teachings of ECK, we have a very pat answer: You do the Spiritual Exercises of ECK. The mainstay is to chant HU, an ancient name for God. You sing HU once or twice a day for ten or fifteen minutes to spiritualize your state of consciousness.

During the time you're singing HU, you are saying to Divine Spirit, "I've opened myself to you. Give me the understanding and the wisdom to meet the waves of life, and the problems, troubles, and whatever else. Give me the strength to meet life." This is basically all that we do when we do a Spiritual Exercise of ECK.

A short session where we meet with the Divine: that is a Spiritual Exercise of ECK.

A short session where we meet with the Divine: that is a Spiritual Exercise of ECK.

THE PASSKEY IS IN YOUR HANDS

When you're ready for something more durable than philosophy, metaphysics, or orthodox religion, then you're ready for the knowledge that grants love, wisdom, and spiritual freedom. These three qualities are available through the teachings of ECK.

The answer is in your hands.

The Spiritual Exercises of ECK are the lost passkey to life. They give the secrets of the ancient ones. A greater state of consciousness is a direct result of doing your spiritual exercises and will reveal new ways to ease your life.

Such freedom is but one of the many benefits that come to all who wish to find the living way and do something about it.

So begins Soul's awakening to the wonder of you!

You are Soul, a child of God. It is your good fortune to eventually become a Co-worker with God. The way of ECK is the single most important choice you can ever make.

And so begins Soul's awakening to the wonder of you!

About the Author

Author Harold Klemp is known as a pioneer of today's focus on "everyday spirituality." He was raised on a Wisconsin farm and attended divinity school. He also served in the U.S. Air Force.

In 1981, after years of training, he became the spiritual leader of Eckankar, Religion of the Light and Sound of God. His full title is Sri Harold Klemp, the Mahanta, the Living ECK Master. His mission is to help people find their way back to God in this life.

Each year, Harold Klemp speaks to thousands of seekers at Eckankar seminars. Author of more than sixty books, he continues to write, including many articles and spiritual-study discourses. His inspiring and practical approach to spirituality helps thousands of people worldwide find greater freedom, wisdom, and love in their lives.

Next Steps in Spiritual Exploration

- **Try a spiritual exercise** on a daily basis.
  Review the spiritual exercises in this book. Experiment with them.

- **Browse our Web site: www.Eckankar.org**
  Watch videos and get more info.

- **Attend an Eckankar event** in your area.
  Visit "Eckankar around the World" on our Web site.

- **Explore an advanced spiritual study class**
  (or study privately) with the Eckankar discourses
  that come with membership.

- **Read additional books** about the ECK teachings.

Advanced Spiritual Study

Advanced spiritual study is available through yearly membership in Eckankar. This annual cycle of study and practice focuses on the ECK discourses, which may be studied privately or in a class. Each year the spiritual student decides whether to continue with his or her studies in Eckankar.

The Easy Way
Discourses

By Harold Klemp

Discourses

As you study the teachings of ECK, you will find a series of changes in your heart and mind that can make you a better, stronger, and more happy person.

Each month of the year, you'll study a new discourse and practice a new technique to enhance your spiritual journey.

The titles of the twelve lessons in *The Easy Way Discourses* by Harold Klemp will give you an overview of the first year of study. The subheads show key subjects and spiritual exercises.

1. The Easy Way

Turning Points • Moving toward ECK • God's Subtle Influence • Learning the Life of ECK • This Month's Exercise: *A technique to meet the Mahanta in full awareness*

2. In Soul You Are Free

The Unique Nature of Soul • To Learn Soul Travel • Set Your Sights on God • Spirit of Adventure • Meet Yourself as Soul • This Month's Exercise: *An easy technique to try for Soul Travel*

3. Dream On, Sweet Dreamer

The Planes of God • The Physical Plane • The Astral Plane • The Causal Plane • The Mental Plane • The Etheric Plane • The Soul Plane • Access to the Inner Worlds • A Doorway to Truth • This Month's Exercise: *A technique for dream travel*

4. Karma—It All Comes Back in the End

Paradise Lost • Karma or Sin? • Sin—A Tool of Control • Cycles of Karma • What Karma Brings Us • Soul Gaining Experience • This Month's Exercise: *A technique for Soul Travel to the Causal Plane*

5. Reincarnation—Why You Came to Earth Again

Cycle of Rebirth • Becoming a Co-worker with God • Learning about Ourselves • Mental Grooves • The Logic of Reincarnation • Peace to a Troubled Heart • You Become More Self-Reliant • Overcome Fear of Death • This Month's Exercise: *A technique to glimpse a past life*

BOOKS

If you would like to read additional books by Harold Klemp about the ECK teachings, you may find these of special interest. They are available at bookstores, online booksellers, or directly from Eckankar.

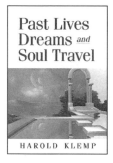

Past Lives, Dreams, and Soul Travel

These stories and exercises help you find your true purpose, discover greater love than you've ever known, and learn that spiritual freedom is within reach.

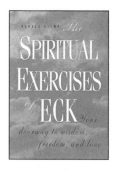

The Spiritual Exercises of ECK

This book is a staircase with 131 steps leading to the doorway to spiritual freedom, self-mastery, wisdom, and love. A comprehensive volume of spiritual exercises for every need.

How to Survive Spiritually in Our Times, Mahanta Transcripts, Book 16

Discover how to reinvent yourself spiritually—to thrive in a changing world. Stories, tools, techniques, and spiritual insights to apply in your life now.

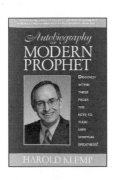

Autobiography of a Modern Prophet

This riveting story of Harold Klemp's climb up the Mountain of God will help you discover the keys to your own spiritual greatness.

Those Wonderful ECK Masters

Would you like to have *personal* experience with spiritual masters that people all over the world—since the beginning of time—have looked to for guidance, protection, and divine love? This book includes real-life stories and spiritual exercises to meet eleven ECK Masters.

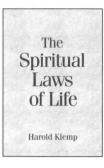

The Spiritual Laws of Life

Learn how to keep in tune with your true spiritual nature. Spiritual laws reveal the behind-the-scenes forces at work in your daily life.

HOW TO GET STARTED

To request information about ECK books or to sign up for ECK membership and get your advanced spiritual study discourses along with other membership benefits (renewable annually), you may:

- Join online at "Membership" at www.Eckankar.org (click on "Online Membership Application"), or

- Call Eckankar (952) 380-2222 to apply, or

- Write to:
  Eckankar, Att: Information, BK87
  PO Box 2000
  Chanhassen, MN 55317-2000 USA

Frequently Asked Questions

What does the word *Eckankar* mean?

Eckankar means "Co-worker with God." It is the destiny of each Soul to experience God and serve all life.

ECK is another word for the Life Force or Holy Spirit, which can be experienced as Light and Sound. It is also known as the Audible Life Stream.

Where did the ECK teachings come from?

The teachings have been on earth since the dawn of human history, in one form or another. No country can claim to be their birthplace.

Many Eckankar terms trace their historical roots to the Far East; however, they have their own meaning and application in Eckankar.

Paul Twitchell made Eckankar known to the modern world in 1965. He separated spiritual truths from the cultural trappings which had surrounded them. Everyday people could now experience the Light and Sound of God while living happy and productive lives.

Many people are looking for spirituality, not religion. They seek experiences, not beliefs. Since Eckankar is a religion, how does it meet these spiritual needs?

Eckankar redefines the experience of religion. It offers an individual the spiritual tools needed to walk one's own journey home to God.

Eckankar gives practical ways for people to have

real spiritual experiences—even the ultimate experience of God—in this very lifetime.

Do the ECK Masters really exist?

The ECK Masters are real.

People from all over the world and from all walks of life have had personal experiences with the ECK Masters years before Paul Twitchell brought them to the public eye.

Many people who have never heard of Eckankar recognize ECK Masters from their dreams and other encounters.

You can read some of these stories and see pictures of some of these ECK Masters on the ECK Masters page at www.Eckankar.org.

Better yet, meet them for yourself. That's the real proof for any spiritual seeker.

The book *Those Wonderful ECK Masters* gives spiritual exercises to help you receive personal guidance from an ECK Master.

How was the current spiritual leader of ECKANKAR, Sri Harold Klemp, chosen?

The Living ECK Master is chosen by God (known in Eckankar as the Sugmad). Every Living ECK Master trains his successor.

In 1981, after years of spiritual training, Harold Klemp became the Mahanta, the Living ECK Master. For more on his background, see "About the Author" on page 105 and the reference to his autobiography on page 111.

What about claims that the modern-day founder of Eckankar, Paul Twitchell, borrowed freely from other authors in writing his Eckankar books?

The golden threads of the ECK teachings had been scattered around the world down through the ages. Some were in books and manuscripts no longer remembered or known by the general public.

Remote writings, little-known truths, and the most accurate parts of what had been given in the past were gathered up by Paul Twitchell—honed, refined, and focused so the public could benefit directly from the pure ECK teachings today.

He was a master compiler. Because of his work and his writings, the ageless teachings of the Light and Sound are now at your fingertips.

Yet Paul's works are only a fraction of the many books of Eckankar. Sri Harold Klemp, the current Mahanta, the Living ECK Master, has authored over sixty books on the teachings since he became the spiritual leader of Eckankar in 1981. His writings are the most current expression of Eckankar.

For more about Paul Twitchell and the history of Eckankar, visit "The Legacy of Paul Twitchell" and the "Paul Twitchell Archive" at the Eckankar Web site (www.Eckankar.org).

Where does Jesus Christ fit into the ECK teachings?

Jesus is viewed as a messenger of God who serves as the spiritual guide for Christians, as spiritual teachers and saints have done for other groups throughout time. Paul Twitchell's book *Stranger By the River* includes passages that speak with beauty and inspiration about the message of love that Jesus brought.

Does Eckankar claim to be the only path to God?

No. While Eckankar offers itself as the most direct path home to God, it does not claim it is the only way to establish a connection with the Divine.

All true religions were created by the Holy Spirit, the ECK, to spiritually uplift humanity.

Is Eckankar a cult?

No.

The ECK teachings are based on compassion, respect, personal responsibility, and giving others freedom. It is against spiritual law to push one's beliefs on others or to hold anyone to a spiritual path.

ECKists take responsibility for their lives, paying their own way and fulfilling their commitments to family, employer, and country. They do not embrace a communal lifestyle. They come from all walks of life and live in the mainstream of society in over 120 countries around the world.

Diet and lifestyle are personal choices.

ECKists respect but do not worship the Living ECK Master. While he is the wayshower and teacher for those who study Eckankar, the individual is fully responsible for his or her own choices and actions in life.

What moral and ethical values does Eckankar stand for?

ECKists believe in personal responsibility for every thought and action. The Law of Karma (cause and effect) teaches Soul right from wrong.

For a moral and ethical compass in everyday life, Sri Harold Klemp has recommended the "Two Laws" distilled by historian Richard Maybury from the ethical, legal, and religious traditions of humanity:

- Do all you have agreed to do, and

- Do not encroach on other persons or their property.

Above these is the high spiritual law—the Law of Love—because God *is* love.

What are the basic beliefs of Eckankar?

Eckankar teaches these basic beliefs:

- Soul is eternal.

- Soul exists because God loves It.

- Soul is on a journey of Self- and God-Realization.

- Soul unfolds spiritually via karma and reincarnation.

- Spiritual unfoldment can be accelerated through conscious contact with the ECK, Divine Spirit.

- Contact with Divine Spirit can be made via the Spiritual Exercises of ECK and the guidance of the Mahanta, the Living ECK Master.

- You can actively explore the spiritual worlds through Soul Travel, dreams, and other spiritual techniques.

- Spiritual experience and liberation in this lifetime are available to all.

Is there a cost or donation for yearly membership in Eckankar?

There is no charge for membership, but there is an annual suggested donation of $130 for an individual or

$160 for a family ($50 for an individual or $75 for a family in developing countries).

What does membership in Eckankar involve?

ECK membership is a yearly cycle of personal study which includes inner and outer spiritual training:

- **Study of the ECK discourses.** These are written by the Living ECK Master and carry a power and wisdom far beyond the written word. These monthly lessons can be studied privately at home, or in a class.

- **Practice of the Spiritual Exercises of ECK,** for about twenty minutes daily. Each monthly discourse gives a new technique to try.

There is no need to make any dramatic changes in lifestyle. The individual continues to live life in one's own unique way, retaining full personal responsibility and choice in everyday life.

Can I practice Eckankar without becoming a member?

Yes. The Mahanta, the Living ECK Master will work spiritually with all who look to him for guidance and protection. However, the ECK initiations are only available for someone who undertakes the spiritual training provided by the Living ECK Master via membership.

GLOSSARY

Words set in SMALL CAPS are defined elsewhere in this glossary.

ARAHATA. *ah-rah-HAH-tah*   An experienced and qualified teacher of ECKANKAR classes.

BLUE LIGHT.   How the MAHANTA often appears in the inner worlds to the CHELA or seeker.

CHELA. *CHEE-lah*   A spiritual student. Often refers to a member of ECKANKAR.

ECK. *EHK*   The Life Force, the Holy Spirit, or Audible Life Current which sustains all life.

ECKANKAR. *EHK-ahn-kahr*   Religion of the Light and Sound of God. Also known as the Ancient Science of SOUL TRAVEL. A truly spiritual religion for the individual in modern times. The teachings provide a framework for anyone to explore their own spiritual experiences. Established by PAUL TWITCHELL, the modern-day founder, in 1965. The word means Co-worker with God.

ECK MASTER(s).   Spiritual Masters who can assist and protect people in their spiritual studies and travels. The ECK Masters are from a long line of God-Realized SOULS who know the responsibility that goes with spiritual freedom.

FUBBI QUANTZ. *FOO-bee KWAHNTS*   The guardian of the SHARIYAT-KI-SUGMAD at the Katsupari Monastery in northern Tibet. He was the MAHANTA, the LIVING ECK MASTER during the time of Buddha, about 500 BC.

GOD-REALIZATION.   The state of God Consciousness. Complete and conscious awareness of God.

HU. *HYOO*   The most ancient, secret name for God. The singing of

119

the word *HU* is considered a love song to God. It can be sung aloud or silently to oneself.

INITIATION.   Earned by a member of ECKANKAR through spiritual unfoldment and service to God. The initiation is a private ceremony in which the individual is linked to the Sound and Light of God.

KARMA, LAW OF.   The Law of Cause and Effect, action and reaction, justice, retribution, and reward, which applies to the lower or psychic worlds: the Physical, Astral, Causal, Mental, and Etheric PLANES.

KATA DAKI.   *KAH-tah DAH-kee*   A female ECK MASTER who, like all others in the Order of the Vairagi, serves the SUGMAD by helping others find the MAHANTA, the LIVING ECK MASTER. Her pet project is to help people get back on their feet during hardship.

KLEMP, HAROLD.   The present MAHANTA, the LIVING ECK MASTER. SRI Harold Klemp became the Mahanta, the Living ECK Master in 1981. His spiritual name is WAH Z.

LIVING ECK MASTER.   The title of the spiritual leader of ECKANKAR. His duty is to lead SOUL back to God. The Living ECK Master can assist spiritual students physically as the Outer Master, in the dream state as the Dream Master, and in the spiritual worlds as the Inner Master.

MAHANTA.   *mah-HAHN-tah*   A title to describe the highest state of God Consciousness on earth, often embodied in the LIVING ECK MASTER. He is the Living Word. An expression of the Spirit of God that is always with you. Sometimes seen as a BLUE LIGHT or Blue Star or in the form of the Mahanta, the Living ECK Master.

PEDDAR ZASKQ.   *PEH-dahr ZASK*   The spiritual name for PAUL TWITCHELL, the modern-day founder of ECKANKAR and the MAHANTA, the LIVING ECK MASTER from 1965 to 1971.

PLANE(S).   The levels of existence, such as the Physical, Astral, Causal, Mental, Etheric, and SOUL planes.

Rebazar Tarzs. *REE-bah-zahr TAHRZ*   A Tibetan ECK Master known as the Torchbearer of Eckankar in the lower worlds.

Satsang. *SAHT-sahng*   A class in which students of ECK study a monthly lesson from Eckankar.

Self-Realization. Soul recognition. The entering of Soul into the Soul Plane and there beholding Itself as pure Spirit. A state of seeing, knowing, and being.

Shariyat-Ki-Sugmad. *SHAH-ree-aht-kee-SOOG-mahd*   The sacred scriptures of Eckankar. The scriptures are comprised of about twelve volumes in the spiritual worlds. The first two were transcribed from the inner planes by Paul Twitchell, modern-day founder of Eckankar.

Soul. The True Self. The inner, most sacred part of each person. Soul exists before birth and lives on after the death of the physical body. As a spark of God, Soul can see, know, and perceive all things. It is the creative center of Its own world.

Soul Travel. The expansion of consciousness. The ability of Soul to transcend the physical body and travel into the spiritual worlds of God. Soul Travel is taught only by the Living ECK Master. It helps people unfold spiritually and can provide proof of the existence of God and life after death.

Sound and Light of ECK. The Holy Spirit. The two aspects through which God appears in the lower worlds. People can experience them by looking and listening within themselves and through Soul Travel.

Spiritual Exercises of ECK. The daily practice of certain techniques to get us in touch with the Light and Sound of God.

Sri. *SREE*   A title of spiritual respect, similar to reverend or pastor, used for those who have attained the Kingdom of God. In Eckankar, it is reserved for the Mahanta, the Living ECK Master.

Sugmad. *SOOG-mahd*   A sacred name for God. Sugmad is neither masculine nor feminine; It is the source of all life.

TEMPLE(S) OF GOLDEN WISDOM. These Golden Wisdom Temples are spiritual temples which exist on the various PLANES—from the Physical to the Anami Lok; CHELAS of ECKANKAR are taken to the temples in the SOUL body to be educated in the divine knowledge; the different sections of the SHARIYAT-KI-SUGMAD, the sacred teachings of ECK, are kept at these temples.

TWITCHELL, PAUL. An American ECK MASTER who brought the modern teachings of ECKANKAR to the world through his writings and lectures. His spiritual name is PEDDAR ZASKQ.

WAH Z. *WAH zee* The spiritual name of SRI HAROLD KLEMP. It means the Secret Doctrine. It is his name in the spiritual worlds.

YAUBL SACABI. *YEEOW-buhl sah-KAH-bee* Guardian of the SHARIYAT-KI-SUGMAD in the spiritual city of Agam Des. He was the MAHANTA, the LIVING ECK MASTER in ancient Greece.

For more explanations of ECKANKAR terms, see *A Cosmic Sea of Words: The ECKANKAR Lexicon* by Harold Klemp.